Dear Eli!

I am Herbert, I am AA
I love you all, isn't it OKAY
I come so fare from Germany
I feel with you and you feel with me
AA is the gratest on this world
you can beleve it boys and girls
15 years I'am a child from AA. hurray
like a free bird in St. Diego sky

Oli yours Herbert
from AA- Germany

Thank you for coming!

:/ Ole = Ole - Ole - Ole -
we are thee children from AA :/.

:/ Ole - Ole - Ole - Ole -
we ar the children OKAY /

Felices 24 horas
Te desea
José Luis Flores
Calle Colón #54
Jerez, Zacatecas
México

AA EVERYWHERE · ANYWHERE

Eli—
So nice to
meet ya!
Dont know ya
But I'll visit S.F.
♡
Alana
7·23·95

AA EVERYWHERE·ANYWHERE

**60th
Anniversary
Celebration
San Diego, California
June 29-July 2, 1995**

Eli
TRUST GOOD
CLEAN HOUSE
& HELP OTHERS
"L·A" MIKE
& K·IT 619 434 8589

Alcoholics Anonymous World Services, Inc.
New York, N.Y.

Photographs courtesy of A.A. Archives.
Material from the A.A. Grapevine is copyrighted
by the A.A. Grapevine, Inc.,
reprinted by permission of the publisher.

Grateful acknowledgement is made to:

Al-Anon Family Group for permission
to reprint from *Lois Remembers*, (pp. 113-14),
© 1979 Al-Anon Family Group Headquarters, Inc.

Parkside Publishing Corp. for permission to reprint from
Grateful to Have Been There, Nell Wing,
(pp. 6-7), © 1992.

ISBN: 0-916856-69-0

Printed in USA

CONTENTS

ALCOHOLICS ANONYMOUS® is a fellowship of men and women who share their experience, strength and hope with each other that they may solve their common problem and help others to recover from alcoholism.

The only requirement for membership is a desire to stop drinking. There are no dues or fees for A.A. membership; we are self-supporting through our own contributions.

A.A. is not allied with any sect, denomination, politics, organization or institution; does not wish to engage in any controversy; neither endorses nor opposes any causes.

Our primary purpose is to stay sober and help other alcoholics to achieve sobriety.

Welcoming Message

It is a wonderful reason to celebrate! Sixty years of this life-saving Fellowship, known throughout the world as Alcoholics Anonymous.

In most cultures, 60 years marks some level of maturity. We hope that along with the joy of sobriety, we have collectively achieved a degree of maturity and a sense of responsibility.

If we view our 60 years in terms of a nation's history, we might concede we are still pioneers—just as at 60 years a nation's citizens were still pioneers. So, along with our maturity and responsibility, we have all the opportunities and challenges that groups of pioneers have always had, plus the knowledge that our mission is a life-saving one.

At this time, whole nations and populations stand in need of our message of hope and sobriety, and our sobriety requires that we carry the message by sharing our experience, strength and hope with other alcoholics. Our primary purpose is still to reach out to the still-suffering alcoholic.

So I welcome you to the 1995 International Convention, celebrating 60 years of sobriety in Alcoholics Anonymous. Enjoy this memorable event, and continue to carry the message—Everywhere and Anywhere.

W.J. (Jim) Estelle, Jr.
Chairperson, General Service Board of Alcoholics Anonymous

Photo Courtesy of James Blank/San Diego Convention & Visitors Bureau

Welcome to San Diego. We meet here to celebrate 60 years of sobriety in Alcoholics Anonymous. At the time of A.A.'s first International Convention, held in Cleveland, Ohio, there were 96,475 members, in 3,527 groups around the world. Today, worldwide membership is estimated at over two million, with approximately 90,000 groups in 141 countries.

THE BEGINNINGS

The origin of Alcoholics Anonymous can be traced to the Oxford Group, a religious movement then popular in the United States and Europe. A well-to-do Vermonter named Rowland H. had visited the noted Swiss psychoanalyst Carl Jung in 1932. Rowland was able to admit that he was "powerless over alcohol" and had decided to attend Oxford Group meetings in New York City. The meetings were

Left: Dr. Carl Jung. Right: Home of Dr. Bob and Ann S., Akron, Ohio.

There have been many changes in A.A. since the last International Convention, held in Seattle in 1990. At that time, the explosion of A.A. in Eastern Europe had just begun. We can remember with great joy the parade of nations at the Big Opening Meeting. That explosion has continued, with an expanded need for written materials in the new and freed nations. There has also been much growth of A.A. in Africa, and the Fellowship is now a true worldwide organization. So have a great Convention! It is our heart-felt wish that this souvenir volume will provide you with a brief overview of our Fellowship, as well as an opportunity to share memories of the next four days with many A.A.s from countries around the world.

held at Calvary Church, under the leadership of the Rev. Sam Shoemaker. At these

meetings, Rowland met an old friend and fellow Vermonter, Edwin (Ebby) T., also

an alcoholic. Through the Oxford Group, they were able to keep from drinking

through a formula of self-inventory, admission of wrongs, making amends, using

prayer and meditation, and carrying the message to

others who still suffered. One of Ebby's school-

William D. Silkworth, M.D.

mate friends was Bill W., also a Vermonter. Ebby sought out his old friend at

182 Clinton Street, in Brooklyn, to carry the message of hope.

Bill W. had been a fair-haired boy on Wall Street, but his promise had been

ruined by continuous and chronic alcoholism. Bill had sought treatment at

The Rev. Sam Shoemaker

Towns Hospital, in Manhattan, under the directorship of Dr. William Silkworth. Bill learned that his problem

was hopeless, progressive and irreversible—that alcoholism caused him to drink against his will, and that it

took only one drink to activate the illness and set him off on a binge of compulsive drinking. Now Bill heard

Ebby's story and once again entered Towns Hospital for treatment. On December 11, 1934, Ebby visited Bill

at Towns Hospital and shared his spiritual journey of recovery. After Ebby left, Bill underwent a powerful spiri-

tual experience. Although not a religious man, Bill experienced the miracle of freedom from the obsessive need

Towns Hospital, New York City

to drink. When he asked Dr. Silkworth about the experience, the "kindly little doctor who loved drunks" did not scoff, but encouraged Bill to "hang onto it."

After Bill's release from Towns Hospital, he began attending Oxford Group meetings. He was buoyed by his contact with other drunks and set out, with little success, to fix all the drunks in the world.

Eventually, Bill got a toehold in his business. In May of 1935, he found himself in Akron, Ohio. In a crisis that many alcoholics can relate to, he found himself alone on a Saturday night in the lobby of the Mayflower Hotel. He was sorely tempted to join the revelers at the bar, but he realized that he needed to share his plight with another alcoholic in order to save himself and protect his sobriety. In an historic decision for A.A.'s future, Bill turned to the church directory in the hotel lobby and began telephoning to try to find another drunk. He reached the Rev. Walter Tunks who, it turned out, knew some members of the Oxford Group in Akron who might help. One of these, Henrietta Seiberling, though not an alcoholic, immediately understood Bill's need and told him of Dr. Bob S., a once-

Church directory in lobby of the Mayflower Hotel, Akron, Ohio.

brilliant surgeon about to lose his practice entirely because of alcoholism. She arranged for Bill to meet Dr. Bob the next day, Mother's Day, at the gatehouse of the Seiberling estate. Dr. Bob, shaking and with a terrible hangover, reluctantly agreed to give this stranger no longer than 15 minutes. Instead of preaching, as he

had done with drunks back in New York, Bill shared his drinking experiences and told Dr. Bob of his own need for communication. He spoke of Dr. Silkworth's insights into the illness of alcoholism.

Dr. Bob, by coincidence, was also from Vermont, and he, too, had already sought help from the Oxford Group. Expecting to

Henrietta Seiberling

hear the rantings of an evangelistic do-gooder, the physician found himself sharing with a fellow alcoholic. They talked for nearly five hours. Dr. Bob "stopped drinking abruptly."

Dr. Bob was to go on one more drunken spree a few weeks later, while at a medical convention in Atlantic City. He had his last drink on June 10, 1935, which is celebrated today as A.A's birth-

Gatehouse of the Seiberling estate.

and Sue. Almost immediately the two men began to try to help other drunks. After some failures, they learned that a patient was in Akron City Hospital for the sixth time in four months and was in bad shape with the D.T.s. They called on him. He was Bill D., a lawyer, who became A.A. Number Three. Soon

Sister Ignatia

182 Clinton St., Brooklyn, N.Y.

day. Bill stayed on in Akron to try to salvage his business deal and, strapped for funds, moved in with Dr. Bob, his wife Anne, and their two children, Bob

Dr. Bob began to treat prospective members on a regular basis at St. Thomas Hospital, with the aid of the indefatigable Sister Mary Ignatia.

Bill returned home late that year and began to call on alcoholics at Towns Hospital. His first success was

Fr. Ed Dowling

Hank P. (who later drank), and slowly a group began to take shape in New York. The first meeting place was Bill and Lois's house on Clinton Street in Brooklyn. They later met at the old 24th Street Clubhouse. Here Bill would eventually meet Father Ed Dowling, who came as a visitor. Father Dowling became Bill's close friend and adviser and one of A.A.'s staunchest supporters.

In 1940, John D. Rockefeller, Jr. hosted a dinner "in the interest of Alcoholics Anonymous." The dinner was held at the Union Club in New York City, and was attended by many of the rich and famous. Bill dreamed of a well-financed global network of drying out stations, with himself as the humble head. He told the story of the low-bottom drunks as only Bill could do. His hopes were dashed when Nelson Rockefeller, pinch-hitting for his ill father, assured the millionaire guests that A.A. was a spiritual program that might be spoiled by money. After the penniless founders recovered from their disappointment, they realized that Mr. Rockefeller had helped them discover that spiritual recovery was more important than money—thus, the principle of self-support had been born!

The Rockefeller dinner also resulted in a much needed wave of newspaper stories. "The effect," said Bill, "was to give A.A. a public status of dignity and worth." It was followed in 1941 by the momentous Jack Alexander article in *The Saturday Evening Post*, which brought Alcoholics Anonymous to national attention, and brought about a new wave of "converts."

In 1938, Bill W. had begun work on the text that was to become *Alcoholics Anonymous*. He attempted to describe "How It Works," and he also included the recovery stories of the early members from New York and Akron. During this process six steps were written, based on the ideas of the Oxford Group. Bill felt that the six steps were essential, but that they had to be expanded in order to "broaden and deepen the spiritual implications of our presentation." In *Alcoholics Anonymous Comes of Age*, Bill tells the story of his hard work and inspiration in writing the Twelve Steps. "There must not be a single loophole through which the rationalizing alcoholic could wriggle out. Maybe our six chunks of truth should be broken up into smaller pieces." In a burst of late-night energy, Bill wrote out the Steps, noting almost by coincidence that the number came to twelve—the same as the twelve apostles. The Steps were included in Chapter 5 of the Big Book after the usual heated debate. In Bill's words, "There were conservative, liberal, and radical viewpoints."

John D. Rockefeller, Jr.

the principles of A.A. for the future. As Bill wrote in *A.A. Comes of Age*: "They represent the distilled experience of our past, and we rely on them to carry us in unity through the challenges and dangers which the future may bring."

The second cornerstone of our Fellowship, the Twelve Traditions, also written by Bill W., were formally introduced at the International Convention in Cleveland in 1950, when the membership voted unanimously to adopt them. Bill and Dr. Bob conceived of the need for the Twelve Traditions as a means of guarding A.A. against itself, and preserving

The Saturday Evening Post, March 1, 1941, containing the Jack Alexander article on Alcoholics Anonymous.

Our Fellowship was very poor in the early days; sobriety was often a fragile and scarce commodity. In 1938, a nonprofit Alcoholic Foundation was formed through the efforts of Dr. Leonard Strong, Bill's brother-in-law. The first Foundation consisted of three nonalcoholic members (Williard Richardson, Frank Amos and John Wood) and two alcoholics (Dr. Bob and a New York member who later drank). Such was the fragile nature of the early membership.

Soon after *Alcoholics Anonymous,* which came to be

Ruth Hock Crecelius, who typed the original manuscript, was presented with the five millionth copy of the Big Book *at the 1985 Convention.*

SERVICE

The Third Legacy

known as the Big Book, was published, the Foundation assumed ownership of Works Publishing Co. The first Foundation office was a cubbyhole at 30 Vesey Street, New York City, staffed by Bill and a nonalcoholic secretary, Ruth Hock, who typed the first manuscript of the Big Book. Ruth also answered many of the thousands of letters for help that began to arrive as A.A. became known.

During the 1940s, Alcoholics Anonymous grew at an almost geometric rate. The Foundation office and the trustees were at the center of the growth, as requests for help flooded the tiny office. The wide use of the Big Book, the expansion of pamphlet literature, pleas for help, and the response to requests for guidance on group problems all constituted a growing service to the world of A.A.

Dr. Harry M. Tiebout was the first psychiatrist to champion Alcoholics Anonymous and to use A.A. principles in his practice. He served as a Class A trustee of the General Service Board.

In 1944, the office moved from Vesey Street to 415 Lexington Avenue, opposite Grand Central Station, where it became a mecca for thousands of A.A. travelers and visitors. As the decade waned, Bill and Dr. Bob saw that the Alcoholic Foundation had no tie to the A.A. membership except through the co-founders. Who would take their place when they passed on? The idea they came up with—selfless and brilliant—was to turn responsibility for the Fellowship over to the Fellowship, to form a service structure through which the A.A. groups would govern their own affairs.

It was proposed that the groups exercise this responsibility by electing delegates who, along with the trustees and office staff, would meet annually. This would be called the General Service Conference. Bernard Smith, a nonalcoholic lawyer who was to serve as the first chairman of the

Gordon Patrick

Michael Alexander

Conference, helped Bill to formulate the Conference Charter. Since several of the trustees and many of

In the early days, a number of dedicated people came into contact with Bill and Dr. Bob. One was nonalcoholic secretary Ruth Hock, who had worked for Bill in the first office in 1936. In a letter written in 1955, Ruth describes the early days:

"By the end of that very first day I was a very confused female for, if I remember correctly, that first afternoon you had a visitor in your office and I think it was Paul K. Anyway, the connecting door was left wide open and instead of business phrases what I heard was fragments of a discussion about drunken misery, a miserable wife, and what I thought was a very queer conclusion indeed— that being a drunk was a disease. I remember distinctly feeling that you were all rather hard hearted, because at some points there was roaring laughter about various drunken incidents. Fortunately I liked you both immediately—I am not too easily frightened—and you were paying $3.00 more per week than I had been getting— so I was willing to give it a try. Somewhere during those first months I also first met Doc S., who gave everyone a feeling of great serenity—peace with himself and God—and an abounding wish to share what he had found with others."

the groups had expressed grave doubts about the new Conference plan, Bill embarked on a personal crusade to sell the idea. In the midst of this effort, Dr. Bob, who had fallen ill with cancer, died on November 16, 1950.

The following year, the first A.A. General Service Conference was held in New York. It was agreed to try the Conference idea for five years to see if it could function as the collective voice and conscience of A.A., yet have absolutely no governing power

A. LeRoy Chipman   Dr. Leonard V. Strong, Jr.

over any individual A.A. member or group. In spite of obvious problems, the General Service Board was named as the replacement for the Alcoholic Foundation at the Second International Convention in St. Louis in 1955.

Bill felt that the final step in the shift of responsibility should be to change the ratio between nonalcoholic and alcoholic trustees on the General Service Board, and he pressed hard for this change for many years. Finally, in 1966, the

Conference recommended that the ratio be changed to seven nonalcoholic trustees and 14 alcoholic trustees (eight regional trustees, four general service trustees and two trustees-at-large). This is the composition of the board today.

Meanwhile, the General Service Office continued to grow. It was to

Bernard B. Smith

Dr. Milton Maxwell

move four more times; it is now located on Riverside Drive and 120 St. Early nonalcoholic secretaries were replaced by A.A. staff members, and a paid general manager replaced the volunteers. Although he had stepped down from active leadership, Bill continued to come to the office one day a week and attend board meetings and Conferences. His health began to fail in the late 1960s; Bill died on January 24, 1971.

Another loving employee was Nell Wing, who still lives in New York City. In her memoir, *Grateful To Have Been There*, Nell writes of her first meeting with Bill.

"So I took the train down to New York City and located an employment agency. The interviewer studied my resume. Then she leaned close and whispered, 'How would you like to work at Alcoholics Anonymous?' Not anticipating my enthusiastic answer, she almost fell off the chair. So it was, on Monday morning, March 3, 1947, a new life began for me when I knocked on the door, on the eleventh floor of 415 Lexington Avenue.

"The next day, Tuesday, Bill W. appeared in the office. His usual pattern then, and to the end of his life, was to spend one or two days a week in town. Charlotte or Bobbie [employees], I'm not sure which, took me over to his desk and left me, saying, 'And this is Bill.' I expected the usual amenities, but, truthfully, I'm not sure he even said hello. He eased his long, lanky frame onto a straight-backed chair, leaned way back, crossed his legs, and immediately launched into a long monologue, talking about how the trustees were trying to keep him isolated in a kind of ivory tower, suggesting he ought to concentrate on just writing for the Fellowship. He went on about the need for something called the Traditions and for a general service conference made up of people from all over the country who would come to New York and help make decisions. I listened with all the interest I could muster, but I didn't really have the vaguest idea of what he was talking about. As I remember, I escaped as soon as I decently could."

THE BIG BOOK

The Big Book, *Alcoholics Anonymous*, is probably the most important single factor in the recovery of most alcoholics who seek sobriety in A.A. It is also one of the nonfiction bestsellers of all time. And yet, it was almost not written.

In 1937, Bill and Dr. Bob met in Akron and tallied the results of their two years' work. They counted together some 40 sober alcoholics, and "saw that wholesale recovery was possible." They agreed that they needed a book that would explain the program to alcoholics and therefore prevent distortion of their word-of-mouth message. Meeting with 18 members of the Akron Group, they proposed the

Bill W. at his desk at "Wit's End," a small studio on the grounds of his and Lois's home, Stepping Stones, Bedford Hills, N.Y.

book. The idea was met with substantial opposition; many were against any publicity, turned thumbs down on any printed material, and argued that "the apostles hadn't needed books." But Bill and Dr. Bob persisted and, "by the barest majority," the Akronites agreed that they should proceed.

By the summer of 1938 Bill had drafted the first two chapters. Harper and Brothers offered to publish the book. But, after much consideration by the trustees of the Alcoholic Foundation and much discussion in the group, it was decided that A.A. should control and publish its own literature—a decision, as it turned out, of tremendous importance for the

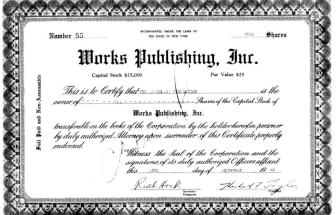

One share of stock in Works Publishing Company cost $25, and could be purchased on the installment plan for $5 a month.

future of Alcoholics Anonymous.

In her memoir, *Lois Remembers*, Bill's wife, Lois, describes the great tension that Bill went through as he wrote the Big Book.

"As Bill finished each chapter, he read it to the group that met at Clinton Street. After these members had discussed it, going over every detail and making suggestions, Bill sent it to Akron for the opinions of members there.

"The pros and cons were mostly about the tone of the book. Some wanted it slanted more toward the Christian religion; others, less. Many alcoholics were agnostics or atheists. Then there were those of the Jewish faith and, around the world, of other religions. Shouldn't the book be written so it would appeal to them also? Finally it was agreed that the book should present a universal spiritual program, not a specific religious one, since all drunks were not Christian....

"When he finished writing and reread what he had put down, he was quite pleased. Twelve principles had developed—the Twelve Steps.

"But when he showed them to the group, the old discussion was resumed. There was 'too much God,' it was said; and 'For pete's sake, take out that bit in Step Seven about getting down on your knees.' They thrashed it out this way and that with Bill as umpire. Finally they hit upon the phrases 'God as we understood Him' and 'a Power greater than ourselves.' These expressions were ten-strikes; they could be used by anyone anywhere....

"Then the question of the

The First Edition of the Big Book, with its red and yellow "circus cover."

title arose. By that time 100 or so members had been sober for two or three years, so the name 'One Hundred Men' seemed appropriate until one woman, Florence, joined the group and objected. 'The Way Out' was very popular for a while, but Bill thought it trite and had Fitz, who was often in Washington, look it up in the Library of Congress. There were already twelve books registered under that name.

"At one time Bill was tempted to call the book 'The W—Movement' (using his last name) and to sign it as author. This natural but egoistical impulse was soon overcome by more mature reasoning."

Finally, the Big Book rolled off the presses in 1939, published under the imprint of Works Publishing. Today, the Big Book—which they could hardly give away in 1939—is available in 30 languages, as well as in Braille and in video in American Sign Language, and is fast approaching a distribution (in English) of 15,000,000 copies.

Volumes of the Big Book in 30 languages.

OTHER AA LITERATURE

By the early 1940s, the General Service Office began to develop service literature for A.A. groups, recovery pamphlets for specific audiences, such as women and young people and public information material for the medical profession.

In 1952, Bill began work on *Twelve Steps and Twelve Traditions*, a set of essays on how A.A. members might apply the Steps and Traditions to their daily life. This book, published in 1953, has become the second largest bestseller in the A.A. catalog.

Bill then turned his attention to the Second Edition of the Big Book. The first eleven chapters remained unchanged, but some of the personal stories were updated. A number of the original stories were dropped, and many new stories were added, to provide more "high bottom" stories. The Second Edition was published in

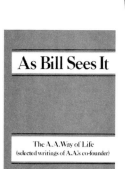

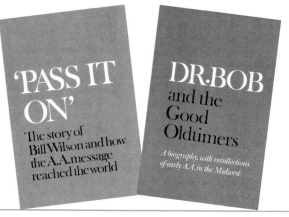

time for the 1955 International Convention in St. Louis. The Third Edition was published in 1976.

The St. Louis Convention provided the material for *Alcoholics Anonymous Comes of Age,* a wonderful history of the first 20 years of the Fellowship. Bill's last book was *As Bill Sees It,* excerpts from his writings, including Grapevine articles and letters. Bill also authored two books of special interest to those involved in A.A. service. The first is the *Third Legacy Manual,* later retitled *The A.A. Service Manual.* He later drafted *The Twelve Concepts for World Service,* which defines the principles of organization for the A.A. Conference. The last two works are now published in one volume.

Today, the General Service Conference initiates literature and, in keeping with the times, audiovisual material. The A.A. message is carried in hard- and soft-cover books; in large print and in Braille; on audio and VHS cassettes. In 1995, the General Service Office expects to distribute nearly 4,000,000 pamphlets, representing 50 titles about A.A. recovery, unity and service.

Most A.A. literature is available in Spanish and French—two languages spoken by many on our continent. Translations into other tongues have been prepared by A.A.s around the world.

THE GRAPEVINE

Through the Years

In the spring of 1944, a New York City A.A. member had what she thought was a crazy idea—publication of a newsletter for A.A. groups in the metropolitan area. A.A. was growing fast and she felt there was a need for greater communication between groups and members. So she took her idea to Bill W., who gave it his blessings. Shortly thereafter, she sat in a coffeeshop talking with two like-minded A.A.s—a writer and a magazine art director—and the idea took shape. As she later recalled, "Over a tough piece of pot roast and muddy coffee, the Grapevine was started on its way...." A couple of similar newsletters had already sprung up in the A.A. communities of Cleveland and Los Angeles, and with these as a guide, the budding editorial staff set out to make their idea a reality.

The first issue came off press in June of 1944. It was an eight-page effort, tabloid size, which sold for 15 cents and featured an article by the prominent nonalcoholic research team of Drs. Howard Haggard and E. M. Jellinek. The issue also included an editorial from Bill W., and shared letters from

The first Grapevines (on left) were in tabloid format. Facsimiles of first issues are available from the Grapevine.

A.A. members who were serving overseas in the Armed Forces during World War II. The issue was distributed free to all groups registered with "A.A. Headquarters" (now known as the General Service Office), and was sent to all known members in the armed services. The idea of the Grapevine slowly caught on, and before long it became known as A.A.'s "meeting in print."

In 1945, the trustees asked the membership if they wanted the Grapevine as the national A.A. magazine. When the answer came back a resounding "yes," the Grapevine was separately incorporated as one of the two service arms of the Alcoholic Foundation (now known as the General Service Board). In order to ensure its editorial freedom and integrity, the Grapevine was designed to be "primarily accountable to the A.A. movement as a whole," and, as Bill wrote in the rough draft of the Grapevine's certificate of incorporation, would be "a newspaper written by A.A.s and friends of A.A. Like the Alcoholics Anonymous movement it is to mirror, there will be but one central purpose: the Grapevine will try to carry the A.A. message to alcoholics and practice the A.A. principles in all its affairs."

The Grapevine has been an integral part of A.A.'s rich history ever since, and has carried important news to A.A. members around the world. The A.A. Preamble originally appeared in the Grapevine in June of 1947, written by the Grapevine's first editor and based on the Foreword to the Big Book. The Traditions were first presented to the Fellowship in the Grapevine through a series of articles by Bill W., and in a December 1950 article,

HI!

"My name is Victor E. and I'm an alcoholic. In July 1995 I celebrate my 33rd anniversary without a drink. Since 1962 I have appeared as a regular cartoon feature in the Grapevine—always hanging around in front of that saloon door—a symbol of victory over alcohol, a day at a time."

Bill and Dr. Bob first suggested that the membership should take over the affairs of A.A. as a whole through the mechanism of a General Service Conference.

At the heart of the Grapevine, however, has always been the sharing of individual A.A. members on topics covering the entire spectrum of recovery, unity and service, and the magazine has reflected the concerns of every generation of A.A.s as they have grown in maturity and sobriety.

Now into its second 50 years, who would've thought back in 1944 that the Grapevine would still be humming along as A.A.'s "meeting in print"— reaching A.A. members in over 70 countries around the world and serving as a timely messenger of A.A. experience, strength and hope?

LONERS AND AAs AFLOAT

"At present I am aboard a ship in the Gulf of Mexico...I pray daily for God's will and His help to keep me calm and avoid resentment. It works. Thank you to all the *LIM* members who participate. I read the *LIM* with joy and gratitude, and your sharing always inspires me." John C.

John is one of the many A.A.s who is cut off from attending meetings by water, land, or circumstances or illness, and for whom it has become necessary to share his experience, strength and hope with other A.A. members by means of print, pen and ink, typewriter, tape, ham radio or computer.

The *LIM* to which John refers is a canary yellow *Loners-Internationalists Meeting* bulletin which is circulated by mail for the asking six times a year and is, in its own words, "an A.A. meeting for Loners, Internationalists, and other A.A.s who cannot attend regular A.A. meetings." It contains many names and addresses, printed confidentially, of solo A.A.s who are eager to correspond with other alcoholics, as

A.A. LONERS-INTERNATIONALISTS MEETING

AN A.A. MEETING FOR LONERS, INTERNATIONALISTS, AND OTHER A.A.'S WHO CANNOT ATTEND REGULAR A.A. MEETINGS

LIM masthead.

well as excerpts from the letters written to the General Service Office in New York, the clearinghouse for this wide-reaching meeting in print. A Spanish-language version of the *LIM* is published in Mexico, and Australia also has a Loners publication.

The first Internationalist was the skipper of an oil tanker named Captain Jack. He discovered A.A. somehow while traveling in the South Pacific during World War II. In 1947, Jack visited G.S.O. in New York City and talked to Bill W. As a result, he set sail with a supply of Big Books, which he left, one at a time, in his wake all around the world. He also had an

Luxury Tanker Brings Us Oil

ODERN EQUIPMENT EASES SEAMAN'S WORK ON U. S. MERCHANT SHIP CARRYING FUEL TO NEW HAVEN FROM TEXAS REFINERIES

New Haven Register
Sunday Magazine

NEW HAVEN 3, CONN., SUNDAY, MAY 24, 1959

On a Socony-vacuum tanker, Captain Jack carried the A.A. message to many foreign lands in the years following World War II, and founded the Internationalists.

address where other alcoholic tars could reach him: the General Service Office. He had thereby started the A.A. Internationalists, as the growing number of sea-going alcoholics plying the international waters and other perpetual peripatetics were henceforth called.

Captain Jack, in fact, lived to attend the first annual, in-the-flesh, Loners-Internationalists Conference in

Akron, Ohio in 1983. He remained at the helm of the A.A. Internationalists until he passed away five years later.

Marty A. from Louisville, Kentucky is a Loner—and not because he wants to be. He writes, "I am going through an extra bad patch physically, and it is making me realize, in a very vivid way, how critical sobriety is to me. As sick as I am, drinking would definitely kill me in a hurry! It also makes me realize how important tools like *LIM* have become to my sobriety...especially on days when the pain is bad. This amazing A.A. program manages to keep my head in the same 24 hours my fanny is in, and, despite everything, that gives some joy and peace in my life."

Loners are isolated from A.A. meetings for any number of reasons: geography, occupation, or, like Marty, physical disability. Homebound folk are also called "Homers." Names and addresses of Loners and Homers, as well as selective parts of their correspondence, are also published in the *LIM*. These days, of course, it is even possible to attend an A.A. meeting just by sitting at your personal computer, if you are on-line and search the right electronic bulletin board, or know a fellow A.A.'s e-mail address.

How many A.A.s participate in the *Loners-Internationalists Meeting* by mail? Estimates vary, but the lives of the people who benefit from it probably number in the thousands. As Loner Ann J. writes—in the middle of a blizzard—from Manitoba, Canada, "My first love is A.A...."

ALCOHOLICS ANONYMOUS IN CANADA

On the map, a border of roughly 3,000 miles separates the United States of America from Canada; within the Fellowship of Alcoholics Anonymous, this imaginary line hardly exists. One yearly General Service Conference, one board of trustees and one A.A. General Service Office in New York City unite the entire North American Fellowship, just as the various national citizenships of the A.A.s at this San Diego Convention are themselves united by the common sobriety every one of us has found in the wonderland of A.A.

Almost immediately after its publication, the First Edition of the Big Book made its way north to Canada. In 1940, a copy fell into the hands of a Toronto minister, the Reverend George Little, a tireless and outspoken temperance advocate at the time. One of his parishioners, who was having "a little trouble holding his liquor," read the copy at the minister's urging. With the Reverend Little's patient encouragement, the alcoholic eventually sobered up, apparently with the Big Book in one hand and the minister holding the other.

In time, the Reverend Little and his now sober friend set out to put into action both their faith and the power of Alcoholics Anonymous to help the recovery of other alcoholics, a church practice called "rescue" in those days. Soon it was called "the A.A. way of living," and George Little had gone down in history as the man who is credited with introducing A.A. to Canada. At the same time, however, small groups of other Canadians also took advantage of a few A.A. meetings in the U.S. by driving across the river from Windsor, Ontario, to Detroit, Michigan.

The Reverend George Little

The Reverend Little and his partner had their work cut out for them. By January 1943, a party of eight — six recovering alcoholics plus the two clerics—gathered for a meeting and dinner at Toronto's Little Denmark restaurant. That number increased at least tenfold by the end of the year. A club room was subsequently opened on Bloor Street, to be replaced later by a then-disused bank building at 1170 Yonge Street. The Yonge Street clubhouse became a well-known and warm A.A. meeting-place in Toronto.

By the end of 1945, A.A. had moved fairly rapidly west into the Prairie Provinces of Saskatchewan, Alberta and Manitoba. The first meeting of record in this region was held at the Winnipeg Psychiatric Institute during the Christmas season of 1944.

In Montreal, Quebec, shortly before World War

II, an ambitious young physician named Travis Dancey tried to interest one of his alcoholic patients, Dave

B., in a life of sobriety. He did not have any luck. By 1944, however, Dave had shown sense enough to read

a copy of *Alcoholics Anonymous*, which his sister in Connecticut had requested by mail from the A.A.

Foundation Office in New York. By study-

ing the Big Book, Dave was able to clean

up his life and his act and stop drinking.

Proudly, he presented himself to Dr.

Dancey and, in short order, Dancey, a non-

alcoholic, and Dave set out as apostles of

the Twelfth Step. Recalled Travis, "He

[Dave] not only dragged me around to

A.A. meetings, but he had the effrontery

to explain the spiritual principles of the

program to me!" Years later, Dr. Travis

The Little Denmark Tavern, where two nonalcoholic ministers met with six alcoholics in 1943, and A.A. in Canada "officially" began. Little Denmark is long gone, but the New York Archives has one of its small red table lamps to preserve that moment in time.

Dancey was elected a Class A (nonalcoholic) trustee of the General Service Board, the first from Canada

Dave B. eventually served as a Class B (alcoholic) trustee, and is remembered by many today as the patriarch of A.A. in Montreal, the center of French-speaking A.A. Quebecois activity.

A.A. meetings conducted in the French language were held in Canada for nearly 15 years before they arrived in France. At present, there are about 1,500 French-speaking A.A. meetings with roughly 35,000 members in the province of Quebec itself. Naturally, they require books, pamphlets and other material in French. These literature needs are met by an organization called Le Service des Publications Francaises A.A. du Quebec, which is responsible for translating Conference-approved printed material from English into French. The French-Canadian version of the A.A. Grapevine is called *La Vigne A.A.*

1170 Yonge Street, handy to the liquor store and railroad station just across the street, was the home of Toronto's beloved A.A. clubhouse from 1944 to 1960.

By 1949, all of the Maritime Provinces—Nova Scotia, New Brunswick, Prince Edward Island and Newfoundland—had been, one at a time, integrated into Canadian A.A. Obstacles were formidable; the weather is quite cold and inclement much of the year, and distances are deceptively great. Newfoundland, for example, is located one-and-one-half time zones from the easternmost tip of the United States, northern Maine.

To the west, where it was virtually untamed and wild for many miles, five alcoholics founded the first A.A. group in Vancouver, British Columbia, in 1944. By 1946, multiple offshoots of their group had grown in Calgary, Chilliwack, across the Straits of Georgia and into Edmonton.

What strikes many as amazing is the fact that this roughly 3,000 mile-border stretches all the way from the Atlantic to the Pacific Oceans, and that A.A. has found its way into just about every bit of settled territory to the north of it. Alcoholics Anonymous is found almost everywhere there are people in the vast Canadian nation. You can find A.A. meetings in the sparsely populated Northern Territories, where colorful vestiges of ancient Eskimo cultures survive to this day.

Because Canada's population is relatively small, considering its land area—compared to that of the United States—many Canadians think little or nothing of traveling hundreds of miles by automobile, motorcycle, snowmobile, air, skis and shanks'mare if necessary, to get to an A.A. meeting, be it just a small group or a crowded Provincial convention.

The spread of Alcoholics Anonymous beyond the borders of the United States was left almost to chance. Or was it the work of the Higher Power, revealed through a magazine article, a visit by a sober, vacationing A.A. member, a physician, a clergyman or members of the Armed Services? A.A. recovery has transcended barriers of geography, language, religion and government; cultures very different from ours have been able to understand the program of Alcoholics Anonymous and assimilate it. As of 1995, A.A. exists—in some fashion—in 141 countries. The situation is extremely fluid, as a visit to an A.A. World Services Board meeting would show. There are

ALCOHOLICS ANONYMOUS AROUND THE WORLD

constant requests for either translations or contributions of existing literature. The most prevalent request by far is for the first 164 pages of the Big Book, with the *Twelve Steps and Twelve Traditions* coming in second.

World Service Meetings, patterned loosely on A.A.'s General Service Conference, share A.A. experience globally. The first World Service Meeting was held in 1967, the brainchild of Bill W., and is now held every two years, alternating between New York City and some international site.

The spread of A.A. around the world was deeply gratifying to Bill W. In May 1950, Bill and Lois went to Europe for the express purpose of visiting A.A. there: Norway, Sweden, Denmark, Holland, France, England and Ireland. And, by 1955, Bill was able to declare, at the St. Louis Convention, that "A.A. had established beachheads in 70 foreign lands." "Beachheads" was what they were, for almost none among them boasted any kind of service office at that time. In the following years, however, Loner members carried the A.A. message to others and formed groups. As the groups multiplied, there came the need to have A.A. literature in their native languages, and to establish some sort of rudimentary intergroup service office. Finally, as the groups grew, both in number and in the geographical area they covered, they felt a need for a structure through which they could manage their own affairs, including a national service office. This chapter provides a few random stories of A.A.'s reception in other countries.

England

In 1947, a traveling A.A.'s need to find fellow members led to the first A.A. meeting in England. The year before, one lone Londoner had quit drinking after contacting G.S.O. in New York; a second had found A.A. in New York, returned to England and contacted the Loner; a third had found sobriety while visiting Bermuda. The visiting A.A. member obtained the three names from G.S.O. and wrote to them in advance, arranging a meeting. Meetings were held regularly thereafter, and by late 1947, the first London group was firmly established, and the first provincial group had been formed in Manchester.

Australia

In Australia, four nonalcoholics read an article by Dr. Harry Tiebout in a psychiatric journal and wrote to the New York office asking for information and a Big Book. One of these men was Father T. V. Dunlea, who had earlier founded Australian Boys' Town. Now he used a similar technique with A.A. In October 1944, in a shack in the bush at Loftus, New South Wales, he held an A.A. meeting with several active alcoholics. The priest had collected them from skid row, and set them up in tents, after the pattern of his Boys' Town. The ragtag group survived.

Rex, one of the founding members of Australian A.A., recalled that the early members latched on to the idea that "sobriety is to be enjoyed, not endured. Some of us being musical, we often varied the A.A. talk with piano, violin and vocal entertainment." Within a few months, the group began public information activities. As a result, the meetings grew to 30 people or more, but they also "became cluttered with philanthropists, social workers, journalists looking for 'copy,' hard-core drunks looking to exploit A.A., and some actual psychotics," according to Rex. The philanthropists were finally told their money wasn't needed; the social workers were told A.A. did its own social work; but the journalists were a problem. In desperation, Rex sat down and wrote a lengthy, well thought-out, authentic account of A.A. and submitted it to the *Sydney Morning Herald.* To everyone's surprise, the paper printed the article. Today, more than 25,000 alcoholics have found recovery in Australian A.A., where public information continues to be regarded as a critical form of Twelfth Step work. Road signs, scattered throughout the country, point A.A.s in the direction of a meeting and let the public know that A.A. is available.

New Zealand

New Zealand proved to be fertile soil for the A.A. seed. Ian M., the drunken black sheep of an affluent Wellington family, tried repeatedly to quit drinking, without success. One day in 1946, on sheer impulse, he checked himself into a psychiatric hospital. There he read the *Reader's Digest* article on Alcoholics Anonymous. He wrote the General Service Office in New

York and received in return a letter and a Big Book. Using the book as an instruction manual, Ian got sober

and sought out other alcoholics. He also passed the good news on to the Wellington Health Department.

Meanwhile in Auckland, a medical doctor was worried about his brother-in-law, Alf, who was about to lose

everything through drinking. The doctor wrote the health department in Wellington, and they contacted Ian.

Ian sent his copy of the Big Book to the doctor, who then took Alf to a cabin 20 miles out in the country and

left him alone for several days with the Big Book. Alf never had another drink!

The Fellowship grew. New Zealand developed a board, a service structure, an A.A. magazine, and a general service office.

Ireland

In 1946, Conor F., an Irish-born A.A. member from Philadelphia, visited

Dublin with his wife. Thus was the beginning of A.A. in Ireland. Three years

sober, Conor brought along four Big Books "just in case." Hoping to plant A.A. in his native land, Conor

went to hospitals, institutions and churches—to be met everywhere with denial, rejection and discourage-

ment. Finally, a Dr. Moore of St. Pat's Hospital understood what Conor was saying and took a copy of

the Big Book to pass along to some patients. None was receptive until he reached Richard P., who became

the first sober member of A.A. in Ireland ("I was glad to find there was one alcoholic in Ireland," Conor remarked!). Conor contacted *The Evening Mail*, which was interested enough to carry an interview and an ad. The newspaper got 30 replies and, as a result, it was decided to have a public meeting. The first Dublin group met November 18, 1946, with 15 in attendance; however, this number soon dwindled down to three. It was at this time that Sackville M. joined. Sackville, dedicated and energetic, was to become the first sober secretary of the group; was responsible for getting A.A. recognized favorably by the Catholic Church in Ireland; made more widely known through newspaper interviews, ads and public meetings; and became editor of *The Road Back*, the Irish A.A. magazine.

Norway

The A.A. story in Norway begins, strangely enough, in a small coffee shop in Greenwich, Connecticut, owned by a quiet Norwegian immigrant, George F., and his wife. George, who had found sobriety in the Greenwich Group, was inspired to write home and tell of his new found life. The response he received from Oslo informed him that his brother was in terrible shape due to alcoholism. George and his wife conferred and decided to sell their coffee shop and go home. Hurrying to the family house in Oslo, they found the brother sick, as had been reported, but obstinately refusing help. When all attempts to help him failed, George and his wife, running out of money, decided to return to America. As they started to leave, the brother called out, "Tell me more about that Alcoholics Anonymous. Explain again their Twelve Steps."

The brother sobered up in time to see George and his wife to the airport. When he returned to his work as a typesetter he started running small ads in the newspaper. Within a few weeks, the wife of an Oslo florist replied, asking for help for her drunken husband, who eventually got sober. When Bill and Lois visited Norway three years later, they were greeted by 50 sober A.A. members!

Finland

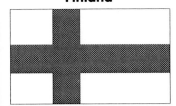

The message reached Finland through a hopeless, broken alcoholic seaman named Usko. Coming off a binge in Los Altos, California, shaking and foggy, Usko was taken to an A.A. meeting by a friend. He never drank again. As his health returned, he had a burning desire to help the drunks back in his native Finland. He wrote a buddy, Veikko K., who he knew was in as bad shape from booze as he himself had been. Unbeknownst to Usko, Veikko was trying desperately to stop drinking by banding together with several other skid-row drunks for mutual support. They met occasionally at the home of a married couple who worked for the Helsinki welfare office. They had fellowship, but no program!

Usko's letter was an answer to a prayer. Veikko says he knew instantly that he could stay sober. He showed the letter to his friends and other Helsinki drunks. Since Usko had no A.A. literature in Finnish to send to Veikko, he continued to write long, long letters week after week, describing the Steps and Traditions

— passing along what he was learning in the Alcoholics Anonymous meetings.

A.A. grew rapidly in Finland. Soon they needed a national service office to handle the mail and phone calls and, eventually, to publish A.A. literature in Finnish. Veikko, dubbed "Kolumbus" because he was the discoverer of American A.A. for Finnish alcoholics, served as secretary of the service office for 36 years. Long before the political changes in Eastern Europe, Finnish A.A.s quietly and carefully reached out to alcoholics in Russia and the Baltics. Today there are more than 15,000 Finns sober through the A.A. program.

South Africa

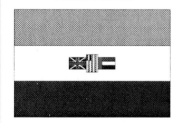

The article in the *Reader's Digest's* international edition also struck a spark in South Africa, and the Big Book lit the flame that started A.A. in that country. In 1946, A.A. started in four separate places in South Africa. In Johannesburg, Arthur S., a successful stockbroker drying out in a posh hospital saw the article and wrote to New York. He received a pamphlet, got sober, and also tried to sober up every drunk with whom he came in contact. In a ghetto at the northern edge of Johannesburg, Soloman, down and out, salvaged a copy of the magazine from a dustbin. He also wrote to New York, who put him in touch with Arthur. And in Cape Town, Pat O'G. also wrote.

However, the recognized founder of A.A. in South Africa is Val D., from Springs. Val went to a priest with his drinking problem. The priest said that he could do nothing, but reached up to a shelf behind him and pulled down what was probably the only copy of the Big Book in all of Africa! One reading struck Val sober, and from this fragile beginning, A.A. began to grow.

Brazil

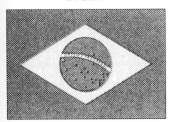

A.A. was carried to Brazil by Herb and Elizabeth D., American A.A. members transferred to Rio on business in 1946. By the next year, they had their "first prospect" and had gotten A.A. front-page publicity in *O Globo*. From the result-ing inquiries, the first group in Brazil was formed and had six members by 1948. There were 81 members in several groups by 1951, and growth continued from there with the help of A.A. literature in Portuguese.

El Salvador

Eddie F., an A.A. member from the United States, is hailed as the founder of A.A. in El Salvador. Eddie sobered up in Boston and had become active in ser-vice before moving to San Francisco where, in 1947, he married a girl from El Salvador. Seven years later they visited her native country. While there, "Mr. Eddie" (as he is universally called in Central America) began carrying the A.A. message. He met only discouragement but kept trying. Finally, and ironically, Eddie's wife told a woman friend about her husband's recovery and a little about A.A.;

the woman asked if Eddie could help her uncle. The latter, who fortunately spoke English, got sober. Thus Don A. became the first link in the chain that led to sobriety for tens of thousands of alcoholics in El Salvador, and the message spread rapidly to other Central American countries.

Mexico

The first A.A. group in Mexico was formed in September 1946 and was made up mostly of English-speaking members. Ten years later, the first Spanish-speaking group was established. As it had previously, the *Reader's Digest* played an important role in exporting A.A.; a '60s article in the Spanish edition brought many requests for help to the General Service Office in New York. These were referred to existing contacts in Mexico. Within a few years, a Spanish translation of the Big Book, plus translations of eight pamphlets, helped carry the message to more Mexican alcoholics. By 1964, there were 36 groups in Mexico, and the first intergroup office was established; within five years, the membership reached 236 and a general service office was established; in 1995 there are more than 15,000 groups throughout the country.

According to Mexico's G.S.O., "women account for hardly 4% of group membership. Focusing on this issue, the 'Message to the Women Committee' encourages and supports the establishment of women's groups and meetings. With this option, more women are now regularly attending group meetings. Today ten areas and three intergroups have committees on carrying the message to women. The Mexican General Service Assembly approved the pamphlet 'Ten Women in A.A.,' which has helped carry the message successfully to women alcoholics."

Iceland

In Iceland, A.A. got off to a very slow start but has exploded in the last 15 years. Gudrun C., an Icelandic woman married to an American and an active A.A. member in New York, visited her home country in 1948 and held a public meeting. As a result, Icelanders were occasionally sent to the U.S. for detox and rehabilitation. When two of these sober alcoholics, Jonas G. and Gudni A., returned to Iceland, A.A. got some publicity — but no group formed. Meanwhile, Gudmunder J., a drunk in Reykjavik, stopped drinking on his own in 1950; when he read Gudni's interview in the newspaper, he contacted him. They got in touch with Jonas G., and on April 15, 1954 (a Good Friday) the first Icelandic group had its initial meeting.

For many years thereafter Iceland had one group whose members stayed sober but engaged in no P.I. or C.P.C. work and little twelfth-stepping. Moreover, there were few pieces of A.A. literature in Icelandic. Then in the early 1970s, the government began an active program of sending alcoholics to the U.S. for rehabilitation. They returned fired up to get A.A. moving and with "revolutionary" ideas of reaching out. Finally, in

1976, the Big Book was published in Icelandic. Explosive growth led to much turmoil, but in the end resulted in the formation of intergroups, a general service office, a board, a conference, and over 200 groups.

Romania

In 1985, the first A.A. group in Romania was started by an American couple. There were many difficulties; the government, fearful of any organization that might act as a cover for subversive activities, forced Grupa Una underground. Within a few years, however, a number of A.A. recovery titles were translated into Romanian by a bilingual member living there. She tirelessly carried the A.A. message, and today there are four groups meeting in Romania. Early in 1995, an English-speaking A.A. member received a supply of Romanian literature. Writing from her home in Arad, she said "please accept a warm thank you from me personally and on behalf of all the other members with whom the bounty will be shared. I can't describe the feeling I got as my father-in-law piled up those cartons of Twelve & Twelve's in my room (he picked them up from the Post Office on his bike), knowing that some day each copy will be in the hands of an alcoholic trying to stay sober. To borrow an expression from the teenagers, 'It was awesome.' The new group in Dena is hanging in there and a second group seems to be on its way in Timisora. *A.A. Comes of Age* has become part of my daily reading and reassures me when one growing pain or another begins to appear ominous, and it is proving true that as long as the fulfillment of our primary purpose is firmly in place none of these growing pains is fatal."

Scotland

The first alcoholic in Scotland to find sobriety through A.A. wrote to New York from Glasgow in 1946, and subsequently found sobriety as a Loner. The following year, a gentleman-farmer drunk from the west of Scotland, near Campbelltown, traveled to the U.S. to attend a Christian conference, hoping to find an answer to his drinking problem. There he met a woman A.A. member who took him to a meeting. Deeply impressed, he quit drinking. After returning to Scotland he began to carry the message into prisons, hospitals, wherever he could find drunks. Later, he was helped in his efforts by an American A.A. visitor. Between these two and the Loner, the first two groups in Scotland were formed in Glasgow and Edinburgh and the message spread from there.

Italy

Italy saw a similar pattern. Although Rome had an English-speaking group in the 1960s, repeated attempts to reach the Italians met only failure. In the early 1970s, a member of their parliament, known as Carlo I., was such a bad drunk that he was in danger of losing his post. He heard of the English-speaking A.A. group in Rome and began attending meetings — even though he did not understand English. The message was carried through an interpreter. Carlo absorbed enough of the program to get sober, stay sober, and carry the message to other Italian alcoholics. This had to be done verbally since there was no Italian literature. He twelfth-stepped Roberto C. and together they spearheaded an effort to publish the Big Book in Italian. This resulted in a virtual explosion of over 100 A.A. groups throughout Italy.

Germany

A.A. began in Germany with American members of the occupation forces. Secrecy was felt to be important and the military A.A. groups met in chapels on military bases, since being an alcoholic was seen as sufficient cause to lose a security clearance. In 1953, members of an A.A. group that met at the army post in Munich went out looking for drunks among the native Germans. They found Max, who became A.A.'s first German member. Thus the first German-speaking meeting began in Munich. By the 1960s a literature distribution center was operating, and a general service office was organized by groups in then-West Germany.

By 1989, the German G.S.O. had become an A.A. address for the people of Eastern Europe, especially those in Germany's eastern sector, plus Czechoslovakia and Hungary. Inge, chair of Germany's General Service Board, observed that "no borders keep out our message, no wall is able to stop it. Beginning in the early 1980s, first with timid contacts, then through literature sent to Loners, and finally through numerous visits between West and East, the ties have been strengthened. Our friends have been waiting for us."

Poland

A.A. in Poland began in 1957 when a Polish physician traveled to the U.S. to learn more about treating his alcoholic patients. Impressed with the success of A.A., he started a group in the city of Poznan when he returned to Poland. That first group remained under the strong influence of the medical profession and ultimately ceased to exist.

In the early 1970s, an alcoholic participating in group therapy was asked by his psychiatrist to translate our newsletter, *Box 4-5-9,* for the group. This project helped get our friend started in A.A. and A.A. started in Poland. A few years later, with financial contributions from A.A.s in Belgium, Canada and the U.S., the Poles purchased a typewriter, producing translations of *Twelve Steps and Twelve Traditions* and *Living Sober.* According to Poland's World Service delegate, "the dynamic development of A.A. in Poland may be attributed in large measure to the priorities established from A.A. literature and to the amount of literature that has been published." In 1995, Poland has more than 800 A.A. groups, with 20,000 members holding meetings in medical dispensaries and clinics; and parish houses and facilities belonging to other associations.

Russia

Over the years, Finnish groups had secretly carried the message across the border to Russian alcoholics. In 1977, 50 Finnish alcoholics took a bus to a Leningrad clinic to speak, only to be told by Russian authorities that their country had no alcohol problem.

By the mid-eighties, with the democratic reforms bubbling up in the then-Soviet Union, and the government's change of heart about alcoholism, A.A. found its way into the Soviet Union, through the visits of individual sober A.A.s from the United States and through a series of exchange visits between American and Russian health care professionals. A.A. was formally invited to participate in the exchange. Moscow saw its first open A.A. speaker meeting on April 14, 1986.

With the political situation radically altered, the U.S.S.R. is no more. In 1995, about 60 groups have started in the republics that once comprised the Soviet Union. There are intergroups in Moscow, St. Petersburg and Volgograd. The All-Russian Society of Alcoholics Anonymous unites A.A. groups in 20 Russian cities and towns and three groups in Lugansk, Lutsk and Donetsk. They have established friendly relations with the A.A. Fellowships of the Ukraine, the Baltics and Byelorussia, all part of the Western Region Intergroup.

A.A. recovery literature and even some public information material have been translated and distributed throughout Eastern Europe — a gift from A.A. members in the United States and Canada. There are books and pamphlets available in Bulgarian, Czech, Hungarian, Latvian, Lithuanian, Romanian, Russian and Ukrainian. One A.A. member recently wrote, "the literature we have received is so dear to us as a newborn baby."

Czech Republic

Slovak Republic

A Loner living in Prague, inspired by the establishment of A.A. groups in Moscow, contacted G.S.O. in New York and asked for help in spreading the A.A. message into what was then Czechoslovakia. G.S.O. New York, in turn, asked the Munich A.A.s to contact the Loner, and a few months later they met with him in Prague. He had arranged visits to several important clinics in Prague, Brno and Bratislava.

The efforts of the Czech Loner, the G.S.O.s in Munich and New York, and the interested physicians all contributed to the establishment of A.A. groups throughout the Czech and Slovak Republics. Translation efforts have begun; the Big Book and some basic recovery pamphlets are available. A Czech A.A. member, writing the New York General Service Office, shared "I am an alcoholic who drank for more than 30 years. Thanks to the fact that the A.A. movement came to our country and I heard about it in 1990, I have not had any alcohol since June 30, 1990. That is unheard of in my case—it is probably even a miracle... everyday I meet plenty of people who need the A.A. program. I believe it is only a matter of time before Alcoholics Anonymous becomes as successful here as it is in the rest of the world."

Japan

In 1947, a U.S. soldier serving with the occupation forces wrote the General Service Office about his plans to start a group in Tokyo. One month later, an article about A.A. appeared in the Pacific edition of *Stars and Stripes,* producing a number of inquiries that were passed along to the soldier. He also spoke to a meeting of enlisted men at a U.S. airfield, with the blessing of the military officials, and registered the first group with G.S.O. in January 1948. This was an English-speaking group, and it would be years before a Japanese A.A. group was formed.

A nonalcoholic physician and hospital director, on a visit to the U.S., had studied the A.A. program and principles and on his return to Japan arranged A.A. meetings for the alcoholic patients at his hospital. The only available literature was in English, which the doctor translated. He also understood the A.A. Traditions to the extent that he kept the group separate from the institution. An A.A. from Fort Wayne, Indiana, stationed in Kobe, wrote the General Service Office, "After seeing this group, I would say that the Japanese are like alcoholics everywhere."

Like our own pioneers, Japan's early members were very active in carrying the A.A. message to suffering alcoholics in hospitals. Akiyo, an A.A. from Tokyo, recalls, "My sponsor told me that on the first day she attended an A.A. meeting, she was sent out to carry the message to alcoholics in a hospital."

There are now about 250 groups, half located around Tokyo and half distributed equally over the other areas. These groups include meetings for young people, for women, and meetings via personal computers.

As part of their 20th anniversary celebration, Japan hosted the Pan Pacific Service Meeting in March 1995. Invitations were sent throughout Asia, plus continents in the Pacific and the islands known as the Pacific Rim: Australia, China, Fiji, Hong Kong, India, Indonesia, Korea, Papua New Guinea, New Caledonia, Philippines, Rarotonga, east coast of Russia, Western Samoa, Singapore, Tahiti, Thailand, Vanuatu and U.S./Canada.

Hungary

In 1980, a German A.A. member contacted medical specialists in Budapest to inform them about Alcoholics Anonymous. Five years later he captured the interest of one of these specialists, whom he invited to attend the annual international meeting of the Bavarian A.A. groups in Augsburg. This doctor then translated the Big Book into Hungarian and sent it to G.S.O. in New York, where it was filed until some A.A. activity developed in Hungary a few years later. Around that time, another physician, who had taken some alcoholism courses in California, gave some A.A. literature to a patient who had been in treatment several times, unsuccessfully. The patient sobered up, visited A.A. groups in Austria and Germany, and returned home to form Hungary's first A.A. group, The Ametiszt (Amethyst) Group, in 1988. Today, Hungary has 35 A.A. groups, stretching from Budapest to the Romanian border.

AA-AN ENORMOUS FIELD OF LOVE

Chapter Five is probably the most famous section of the Big Book. Its first few pages are read aloud at the start of many, many Alcoholics Anonymous meetings. Its title is "How It Works."

Since the earliest days of the Fellowship, when someone, whether a member or not, has asked of an A.A., in good faith, "How does it work?" the facile, conventional answer has usually been, "Fine! A.A. works just fine."

This classic Q and A is obviously a dodge: fancy footwork worthy of the late Mr. Fred Astaire. The question, in fact, may be impossible to answer; and any answer, in all likelihood, does not really address

Name _____

Telephone _____

BIKERS

If you drink, that's your business. But if you want to quit and can't, then it's our business.

Card handed out at 1985 Convention in Montreal by Fifth Chapter A.A. members.

the question. Nevertheless, the response, "Fine! A.A. works just fine," is about as close to the truth as anyone has gotten to date. Chalk one more paradox up to the miracle of A.A.

Indeed, A.A. does seem to work "just fine" everywhere — except in those places on the globe (are there some?) where there are no alcoholics! Age, sex, nationality, race, language and all of the differences in cultures that seem to divide both people and nations do not divide A.A. members one from the other. Strangely, they appear to bring A.A.s closer together. Traditional enemies have often been united by a common desire to help one another to recover from the illness of alcoholism.

A German A.A. named Alfred put it this way: "Unity can be illustrated by an A.A. meeting held in Haifa, attended by a Palestinian man from Jerusalem, a Jewish man from Gaza, a 'hippie' girl from San Francisco, a 'punk' from Berlin, a new immigrant from Russia, a Shiite from Lebanon, a pair of tourists, a man and a woman from Finland. Most of them speak only a little English. All are happy, because all are standing on their native soil, in the A.A. Fellowship. A.A. is an enormous field of love, where the anarchy of the spirit can be transformed into the democracy of recovery. A.A. unites nations. Most of all, A.A. unites people."

If Alcoholics Anonymous were a gigantic department store, the sign in the enormous glass window might proclaim in a multitude of languages, "Here is spoken the Language of the Heart."

Put another way, Roberto from Mexico is direct and eloquent: "Once, when I was talking with my sponsor about how privileged we are to be members of A.A., we started to think about how, out of tens of millions of alcoholics there are in the world, we managed to find ourselves among the two million fortunate alcoholics who experienced the joy of living with-

out alcohol. You could say that we were the two million survivors of the eternal shipwreck that alcoholics have

suffered, swallowed up by the raging sea of alcoholism. It is our good luck to have been born in the age of

Alcoholics Anonymous, rather than in some past century, when there was hardly any hope of escaping the

clutches of alcohol."

Chapter 5

HOW IT WORKS

RARELY HAVE we seen a person fail who has thoroughly followed our path. Those who do not recover are people who cannot or will not completely give themselves to this simple program, usually men and women who are constitutionally incapable of being honest with themselves. There are such unfortunates. They are not at fault; they seem to have been born that way. They are naturally incapable of grasping and developing a manner of living which demands rigorous honesty. Their chances are less than average. There are those, too, who suffer from grave emotional and mental disorders, but many of them do recover if they have the capacity to be honest.

Our stories disclose in a general way what we used to be like, what happened, and what we are like now. If you have decided you want what we have and are willing to go to any length to get it—then you are ready to take certain steps.

At some of these we balked. We thought we could find an easier, softer way. But we could not. With all the earnestness at our command, we beg of you to be fearless and thorough from the very start. Some of us have tried to hold on to our old ideas and the result was nil until we let go absolutely.

Remember that we deal with alcohol—cunning, baf-

Capítulo 5

COMO TRABAJA

A vez hemos visto fracasar a una persona que haya uido concienzudamente nuestro camino. Los únicos recuperan son los individuos que no pueden, o no tregarse de lleno a este sencillo programa; general- hombres y mujeres incapaces, por su propia natu- er honrados consigo mismos. Hay seres desventu- éstos. No son culpables; por lo que parece, han r su naturaleza, son incapaces de entender y de do de vida que exige la más rigurosa honradez. s probabilidades de éxito son pocas. Existen e sufren graves trastornos emocionales y men- muchos de ellos logran recuperarse si tienen iente para ser honrados.

torias expresan de un modo general cómo s aconteció y cómo somos ahora. Si tú has eres lo que nosotros tenemos y estás dis- o lo que sea necesario para conseguirlo, en- diciones de dar ciertos pasos.

sistimos a algunos de ellos. Creímos que r un camino más fácil y cómodo. Pero no que, con todo el ahínco que pueda ani- s que seas valiente y concienzudo desde zo. Algunos de nosotros tratamos de nuestras viejas ideas y el resultado fue nulo hasta que nos deshicimos de ellas sin reserva.

Recuerda que tratamos con el alcohol: astuto, desconcer- tante y poderoso. Sin ayuda resulta demasiado para nosotros.

Chapitre cinquième

NOTRE MÉTHODE

nnaissance, rares sont ceux qui ont a appliquant pleinement notre méthode. t pas rétablis sont des gens qui ne peu- lent pas s'engager pleinement dans ce et ce sont d'habitude des hommes et r leur nature, sont incapables d'être mêmes. Il y a de ces malheureux. Ce ils semblent nés de cette façon. De bles d'adopter et de cultiver un style ureuse honnêteté. Dans leur cas, la t au-dessous de la moyenne. Il y a ctés de graves désordres émotifs et mbre, plusieurs peuvent en fait se s d'être honnêtes.

s révèle globalement ce que nous vé et ce que nous sommes main- enus à la conclusion que vous ue nous avons, et si vous êtes rien pour l'obtenir, vous voilà apes.

nt pas manqué de nous rebu- es moyens plus faciles, moins rien trouvé. En y mettant es capables, nous vous sup- vec courage et application. vé de composer avec leurs en fait qui vaille tant qu'ils n.

s affaire à l'alcool, un nt! Sans aide, c'est trop

"The miracle of A.A.," writes Jean in Colorado, "is not that I am sober; any fool can stay sober, if he or she doesn't drink. The miracle of A.A. is that I do not want to drink any more."

How does A.A. work? Why does A.A. work? These shopworn questions have provided hours of coffee-cup disputation for six decades—and let us hope they continue to for at least sixty more. Listen to George in South Africa, who offers two clues. They are both only clues—good clues but not solutions to the old mysteries. "I was alone in the world and was filled with despair and, as was true for so many of us, more than a fair share of regret, remorse, fear and loneliness," says George. "In A.A., I found myself among a group of people to whom it did not matter who I was or what I was. What mattered was that I had a desperate need to do something about my drinking problem in my life. What a blessing! The only requirement for membership was a desire to stop drinking. This proved to be, and, in my opinion, remains one of the cornerstones of our Fellowship. No one stood in judgment of me. So often, what is heard at A.A. meetings is 'this is what I did,' rather than 'this is what you ought to do.'"

In other words, first we wanted to stop drinking and start living. Second, we wanted to stand on the "enormous field of love" and join hands.

Or, as the wiseacre, Frank, of New York City, sums it up: "The disease isn't contagious, but the recovery is."

The proof is all around us here in San Diego.

AA IN CORRECTIONAL FACILITIES

November 28, 1943, is a little-known landmark day in A.A. history. Bill W. himself was the guest speaker at an A.A. meeting held in California's then notorious San Quentin Penitentiary. The famous warden, Clinton Duffy, had allowed the first A.A. meeting to be held at that prison in 1942, and Bill was anxious to observe the progress of this unprecedented step.

"There were formidable problems to solve," Bill wrote later, "but Warden Duffy took them, and his faith was justified."

The fact that the majority of criminal acts committed in North America occur after the perpetrator has been drinking (usually heavily) is reason enough for the fact that A.A. meetings in prisons and jails for both men and women are now the rule rather than the exception, not only in the United States and Canada, but around a good deal of the globe. Although he or she may not be inclined to boast about it, a good number of A.A.'s most active members attended their first A.A. meeting while serving time in a jail or prison.

Approximately 500 letters a month arrive at the General Service Office from prisoners who may request literature or ask for information about starting a new group, advice regarding group disputes or help in making contacts with outside A.A. sponsors. Local institutions committees, which have increased in number considerably during the past decade, are often encouraged by correctional officials to bring speakers to prison meetings from outside the walls, especially A.A. members who, at one time or another, have served time themselves. Inmates are almost always grateful for this secondhand taste of a free life and the living reminder of the opportunity for a sobriety that awaits the majority of them, a day at a time, upon parole or release.

Warden Clinton Duffy

Many "outside" A.A.s also do Twelfth Step work by volunteering for the Corrections Correspondence Service. G.S.O.'s Correctional Facilities coordinator matches up inmate requests for outside correspondents with A.A.s wishing to correspond with A.A.s on the "inside."

Also, local area Correctional Facilities committees often set up networks of prerelease contacts so inmates will have immediate contact with A.A. in the area where they will settle after incarceration.

A completely reliable estimate of the number of A.A. members in correctional institutions today in North America is impossible to make, but the number of A.A. member inmates in detention facilities probably lies somewhere in the vicinity of 51,000. At any rate, G.S.O.'s Correctional Facilities desk records 2,085 groups presently meeting in penal institutions of various sorts in the U.S. and Canada in 1995. Most of them have full status as bona fide, recognized, regular A.A. groups, and, incredibly, about a dozen of them have made recent contributions to G.S.O.'s General Fund. "The language of the heart" is spoken everywhere.

AA IN TREATMENT FACILITIES

Helping a newcomer to bridge the gap between the cocoonlike life in a hospital or treatment center and be-coming a sober, active member in the Fellowship is possibly the oldest, and one of the most critical, challenges Alcoholics Anonymous holds out to any of its members.

The story of how, in 1935, Bill W. and Dr. Bob S. visited A.A. number three, Bill D.—known as "the man on the bed"—in an Akron, Ohio, hospital has become a Fellowship legend. Dr. Bob's Herculean Twelfth-Step activities at St. Thomas Hospital before his death in 1950 is another. So spectacular were the thousands of re-coveries attributed to Dr. Bob and nurse Sister Ignatia, that Bill frequently referred to his co-founder as "the Prince of twelfth-steppers."

Barely sober alcoholics today may come from one of a number of different sorts of institutions, after which they are encouraged to start working the A.A. program as soon as possible. For many, this is not quite as sim-ple as it sounds. Where do they go? What do they do? Whom can they trust?

For this reason, A.A. members are encouraged at all levels—local, state and area-wide—to participate in one of the more than 400 Treatment Facilities committees that are presently in contact with the Treatment Facilities desk at the General Service Office. It is highly probable, however, that many A.A. members on the group level also work silently and anonymously in their own communities in helping newly "dry" alcoholics at small treatment facilities. Such treatment centers have become nearly ubiquitous in the past decade, as have hospital programs where alcoholics remain after detoxification.

These local T.F. committees are designed to help alcoholics in any kind of treatment program, even the shortest, to make the tricky transition from a regulated environment to the real world, with all of its temptations, beyond its front door. Experience has shown that one of the most slippery paths in the world is that short one between an alcoholism treatment center and a local cocktail lounge, gin-mill or liquor store.

One time-honored way of doing this is to hold Beginners Meetings at the facility itself. The practice usually permits A.A. members who are successfully recovering in the A.A. Fellowship to serve as powers of example for the usually skeptical, shaky patients—most of whom are uncertain about whether they want sobriety in the first place, and how to find it, if they do.

St. Thomas Hospital, Akron, Ohio, the first "detox."

It is also a splendid opportunity for A.A. members to answer specific questions that patients harbor about any aspect of the A.A. Fellowship and to distribute literature that may not be available at the facility.

Another function of these committees is to offer the Temporary Contact Program, which is designed to help a patient who is newly released from a treatment program to negotiate that difficult road between the facility and his or her first A.A. meeting—followed, one hopes, by membership in Alcoholics Anonymous.

To this end, volunteer A.A.s serve as temporary contacts for the newcomer, thereby insuring that the neophyte attends a variety of meetings, recognizes the value of joining a home group and is helped to overcome any shyness he or she may display when talking to A.A. members.

AA AND COOPERATION WITH THE PROFESSIONAL COMMUNITY

According to a recent A.A. Membership Survey, more than half of our new members these days have been introduced to the Fellowship by a so-called "outside source": a professional alcoholism counselor or one of many individuals trained to utilize A.A. as the most effective resource yet developed to help drunks find their way back to productive lives.

These professionals give medical, spiritual, psychological, or other counseling advice that requires an accurate understanding of what A.A. is and how it works. They also need to know what A.A. members can and cannot do in helping the alcoholic who is still active. This is the main function of our Fellowship's

Cooperation With the Professional Community (C.P.C.) desk at the General Service Office.

Dr. John L. Norris, associate medical director of the Eastman Kodak Company, had, as early as 1948, begun investigating A.A. as a resource available to help alcoholic employees at Kodak's plant in Rochester, N.Y. "Dr. Jack," as he later became known in A.A., liked what he saw. He eventually served as Class A (nonalcoholic) chairman of the General Service Board of Trustees of A.A. for many years, and upon leaving that post became a trustee emeritus. One of Dr. Jack's favorite sayings was, "Sponsor your doctor." We can expand that to include our lawyer, clergy, therapist, police chief and friends.

Dr. John L. Norris

We also need to support actively local, area and national professional community efforts at providing for the still-suffering alcoholic an opportunity to learn what the Fellowship of Alcoholics Anonymous is and to see, firsthand if possible, the miracles it can accomplish.

When we "carry the message" of A.A., we are not referring only to one alcoholic talking with another, however rewarding we feel that a flesh and blood handclasp, always ready to help someone in need, may be. We also "keep it by giving it away," when we cooperate with our professional friends, alcoholic or nonalcoholic. Helping them is Twelfth Step service, just as surely as the old-fashioned but somewhat more traditional, person-to-person, voice to ear communication is.

Sometimes, as the result of our own experiences, we may become a bit selfish—even egotistical—in thinking that we alcoholics are the only ones who can talk productively to another alcoholic. We often need to let go of this self-centeredness and recognize that quite frequently a nonalcoholic professional may have an opportunity that is not open to us to steer a drunk to the A.A. Fellowship. The all-important result is that the body gets there, not who brought it.

Our Cooperation With the Professional Community desk, supervised by a G.S.O. staff member, functions as a two-way street to keep the traffic flowing between an ever-growing number of professionals concerned with the illness of alcoholism and A.A., both in the interests of all of us in the Fellowship and of our communities, large and small, that we, as recovering alcoholics, are proud to serve.

AA AND PUBLIC INFORMATION

Co-founder of Alcoholics Anonymous Bill W. was acutely aware of the necessity of publicity in and about A.A. At the same time, he recognized the dangers of the contradiction of generating public information about a fellowship that relied, in large part, upon the spiritual principle of anonymity for its success.

Wrote Bill, "Public Information takes many forms—the simple sign outside a meeting place that says 'A.A. Meeting Tonight'; listings in local phone directories; distribution of A.A. literature; and radio and television

shows using sophisticated media techniques. Whatever form, it comes down to 'one drunk carrying the message to another drunk,' whether through personal contact or through the use of third parties and the media."

With the assistance of the Public Information desk at G.S.O., Public Information committees at the area, group and intergroup/central office levels are encouraged, wherever possible, to carry the A.A. message to the general public in schools, industry, service organizations and in the mass broadcast and print media. To this end, Public Information committees may arrange community gatherings, send speakers to psychology or sociology classes at local colleges or provide speakers for civic groups. A.A. members may even be asked to join panels on alcoholism at well-known medical schools. Of course, Public Information committees are always ready to help radio and television broadcasters. They make themselves available to filmmakers whenever their screenplays treat recovery in Alcoholics Anonymous. P.I. committees are also responsible for developing A.A.'s own radio and television short "spots" and public service announcements in various languages, produced both by the General Service Office and other P.I. committees in the U.S. and Canada.

On the other side of the coin, however, it is also the unique task of Public Information committees to safeguard the Twelve Traditions of the A.A. Fellowship, particularly those that relate to anonymity or affiliation with outside organizations. Should problems occur, usually a polite suggestion, via mail, phone call or in person, clears up the difficulty, which, more likely than not, resulted from some kind of misunderstanding.

It has long been a custom for G.S.O. to send an annual letter to media contacts working on newspapers and magazines and in the world of broadcasting to remind them of A.A.'s Tradition of Anonymity and its significance. In recent years, more than 4,000 such letters have been mailed to influential print and broadcast personnel each year.

INTERNATIONAL CONVENTIONS

15th Anniversary, 1950 — *The First A.A. International Convention, Cleveland, Ohio*

The crowd of thousands (no accurate figure exists) voted to accept from the founders A.A.'s Legacy of Unity, and the Twelve Traditions assuring that Unity. The Convention program was remarkably like today's! It included A.A. for women, A.A. in industry, young people in A.A., and A.A. in correctional institutions. There was a Spiritual Meeting Sunday morning and a Big Meeting on Saturday night, where Dr. Bob gave his last talk and Bill reported on the growth of the Fellowship. It even closed with "A Vision for You"! The Convention was termed "international" because Canadian members were present.

20th Anniversary, 1955 — *St. Louis, Missouri*

A.A. "Came of Age" as the assembled crowd accepted from the

founders the Third Legacy of Service (i.e., the Service Structure and the Conference). The proceedings of those three days are reported in *A.A. Comes of Age*. Among the many early A.A. friends present were Father Ed Dowling, Rev. Sam Shoemaker, Dr. John L. Norris, Bernard Smith and Dr. Harry Tiebout. Bill and Lois were there, of course. The General Service Conference was a part of the Convention, with all the delegates on stage for the Sunday morning meeting. The second edition of the Big Book was introduced. President Dwight D. Eisenhower sent a telegram. The "official" attendance was 5,000.

25th Anniversary, 1960 — *Long Beach, California*

Notable at this silver anniversary Convention was the number of historic figures who were present: Bill and Lois, Sister Ignatia, Judge John Murtagh, Col. Edward Towns, Leonard Harrison, Marty M., Warden Clinton Duffy, Archie Roosevelt, Dr. John L. Norris, Dr. Harry Tiebout, and a host of early A.A. members. Bill gave one of his most memorable (and longest!) talks. The Big Show featured a parade of Hollywood stars and celebrities such as

Peggy Lee, Jayne Mansfield, Dennis Day, Buster Keaton, and Les Brown & His Band of Renown. This gathering set the format for International Conventions to follow—8,700 registrants filled the meetings. No wonder Long Beach ran out of coffee!

30th Anniversary, 1965 — *Toronto, Ontario, Canada*

Who can forget the owning of the Responsibility Declaration by the 10,000 members and their friends massed in the Maple Leaf Gardens? The major talks were still made by Bill and Lois, and Bernard Smith. Dr. Jack was everywhere. Overseas attendance was growing. The film "Bill's Own Story" was introduced. New names among the nonalcoholic speakers were Selden Bacon, from the Rutgers School on Alcohol

Studies; Dr. Marvin Block, of the American Medical Association; the Rev. Howard Clinebell; and Dr. Luther Cloud.

35th Anniversary, 1970 — *Miami, Florida*

Co-founder Bill, terminally ill by this time, made a last surprise appearance at the Sunday morning Big Meeting before a weeping, cheering audience of 10,900 people. Bernard Smith also made his last talk. New nonalcoholic figures included Dr. Max Weisman, Archer Tongue, Dr. Stanley Gitlow, Dr. Vincent Dole. Dr. John L. Norris was still the dominant leader. President Richard Nixon wired congratulations. The film "Bill Discusses the 12 Traditions" was introduced. "A.A. Around the World" acquired real meaning as foreign tongues abounded.

40th Anniversary, 1975 — *Denver, Colorado*

A crowd of 19,800 surpassed the wildest expectations, overflowing Currigan Hall into the Sports Arena across the street, where the Big Meetings were carried by closed-circuit television. Workshops and panel meeting

rooms were so jammed that the fire department repeatedly closed down the attendance. The Flag Ceremony

was held for the first time (29 countries represented) and there wasn't a dry eye in the house! The theme "Let

It Begin With Me" was spoken by every flag bearer in his own language, and was sung by Debbie M. President

Gerald Ford sent greetings. The world's largest coffee-maker produced a half million cups a day.

45th Anniversary, 1980 — *New Orleans, Louisiana*

An elaborate Mardi Gras parade on Thursday evening launched the festivities. Over 22,500 registrants,

plus families and friends, filled the Superdome for the Big Meetings, which were translated simultaneous-

ly into French, Spanish, German and English. Celebrating the theme, "The Joy of Living," 33 countries

participated in the Flag Ceremony. A.A.s took over the town with the largest number of meetings ever

(as many as ten concurrently), and famed Bourbon Street turned into "Ice Cream and Coffee Street" as

A.A. overran it! We had the first true Marathon Meeting, where a nameless drunk off the street sobered

up and appeared at the Sunday Spiritual Meeting! An unforgettable moment came when a stranger told

the crowd, "I am probably the only person here who was present when Bill met Dr. Bob!" It was Dr.

Bob's only son!

50th Anniversary, 1985 — *Montreal, Quebec, Canada*

In the United States it was the 4th of July weekend, but it was an "independence day" of a different kind for the more than 45,000 members of A.A. and Al-Anon and their families, who arrived in Montreal, Quebec, Canada, sober and free of the illness of alcoholism. It was the largest number of drunks ever assembled anywhere, celebrating Alcoholics Anonymous's first half-century. Hotels in the beautiful French-Canadian metropolis were so packed that some participants roomed 75 to 90 miles out of town! Fifty-four countries marched in the Friday night Flag Ceremony at the Olympic Park Stadium. Ruth Hock, who as Bill W.'s secretary had typed the original Big Book manuscript, received the five millionth copy of the Big Book. Many of those with time for sightseeing enjoyed exploring Old Montreal, a unique restoration along the St. Lawrence River. Participants found plenty of opportunity for sober fun on this historic weekend in this lovely, bilingual, clean and colorful setting!

55th Anniversary, 1990 — *Seattle, Washington*

They came by plane, train, ship, bicycle and covered wagon, from 75 countries, a number of them representing nations that had once been part of the U.S.S.R. A.A.'s 1990 Convention in Seattle was not only the largest to date—with registration at 48,000—but the largest convention ever hosted by Seattle. The local Seattle A.A. Host Committee alone was more than 3,000 strong! A marathon candle, symbolically lighting the way to sobriety for the still-suffering alcoholic, burned from Thursday midnight to Sunday morning. Nell Wing, Bill's longtime secretary and A.A.'s first archivist, headed home with the ten millionth copy of the Big Book, presented to her in the Kingdome Stadium to a deafening ovation.

60th Anniversary, 1995 — *San Diego, California*

A Thursday night "Block Party" right outside of the San Diego Convention Center and along the waterfront to the Seaport Village area provides the setting for A.A.'s celebration of its 60th Anniversary. The theme, "A.A. Everywhere—Anywhere," translates into A.A. sharing in a multitude of ways, such as workshops, mini-marathons and Mammoth Meetings at the Jack Murphy Stadium. Include as well in the celebration the heart-warming Saturday Oldtimers Meeting—to say nothing of the harbor city's many beachside and other salt-air attractions and its famous zoo.

San Diego Convention Center

The Twelve Steps
of Alcoholics Anonymous

1. We admitted we were powerless over alcohol—that our lives had become unmanageable.

2. Came to believe that a Power greater than ourselves could restore us to sanity.

3. Made a decision to turn our will and our lives over to the care of God *as we understood Him.*

4. Made a searching and fearless moral inventory of ourselves.

5. Admitted to God, to ourselves and to another human being the exact nature of our wrongs.

6. Were entirely ready to have God remove all these defects of character.

7. Humbly asked Him to remove our shortcomings.

8. Made a list of all persons we had harmed, and became willing to make amends to them all.

9. Made direct amends to such people wherever possible, except when to do so would injure them or others.

10. Continued to take personal inventory and when we were wrong promptly admitted it.

11. Sought through prayer and meditation to improve our conscious contact with God, *as we understood Him,* praying only for knowledge of His will for us and the power to carry that out.

12. Having had a spiritual awakening as the result of these steps, we tried to carry this message to alcoholics, and to practice these principles in all our affairs.

The Twelve Traditions
of Alcoholics Anonymous

1. Our common welfare should come first; personal recovery depends upon A.A. unity.

2. For our group purpose there is but one ultimate authority—a loving God as He may express Himself in our group conscience. Our leaders are but trusted servants; they do not govern.

3. The only requirement for A.A. membership is a desire to stop drinking.

4. Each group should be autonomous except in matters affecting other groups or A.A. as a whole.

5. Each group has but one primary purpose—to carry its message to the alcoholic who still suffers.

6. An A.A. group ought never endorse, finance, or lend the A.A. name to any related facility or outside enterprise, lest problems of money, property, and prestige divert us from our primary purpose.

7. Every A.A. group ought to be fully self-supporting, declining outside contributions.

8. Alcoholics Anonymous should remain forever non-professional, but our service centers may employ special workers.

9. A.A., as such, ought never be organized; but we may create service boards or committees directly responsible to those they serve.

10. Alcoholics Anonymous has no opinion on outside issues; hence the A.A. name ought never be drawn into public controversy.

11. Our public relations policy is based on attraction rather than promotion; we need always maintain personal anonymity at the level of press, radio, and films.

12. Anonymity is the spiritual foundation of our traditions, ever reminding us to place principles before personalities.

To Dear Eli
What a Wonderful and
beautiful life this is
— Thank you for being
part of mine
Love Suresh
Johanesburg S. Africa
27 (011) 462-5952

Easy does it

Agir aisément

Tomalo con calma

Keep it Simple

Vivre et laisser
vivre

Lo primero,
primero

First things First

**Par la grâce
de Dieu**

**Piensa, Piensa,
Piensa**

Think, Think, Think

Garde ca Simple

Déjalo en manos
de Dios

Live and Let Live

L'important d'abord

Manténlo Simple